LEARN TO PROGRAM WITH C#
YOUR TICKET TO A BRIGHT FUTURE

QODE CAMP

———————

Andy V

PROGRAMMING C#: YOUR TICKET TO A BRIGHT FUTURE

Copyright © 2023 by QODE CAMP/ANDY V

All rights reserved. No part of this book may be reproduced or transmitted in any form or by any means without written permission from the author.

ISBN: 9798372584358

If you need to contact us, please email:
support@qodecamp.com

The video series will soon be available for purchase on QodeCamp.com, and by following along with the series, you will be able to facilitate and streamline your learning experience.

Feedback and improvement suggestions are welcome!

DEDICATION

Dear Mom,

I dedicate this book to you, the woman who has always been my biggest supporter and cheerleader. You were there for me from the moment I was born, always putting my needs before yours. You made countless sacrifices to give my brother and me a happy, loving childhood, and you were always there to lend an empathetic ear when I needed to talk or to offer guidance when I needed it.

Even though you are no longer with me, the memories of your love and support will stay with me forever. You may be gone, but the void you have left will never be filled. You are always in my thoughts and in my heart.

Thank you for everything you did for me, Mom. I am who I am today because of all that you have done for me. You will always be my hero.

With all my love,
Andy

TABLE OF CONTENTS

Chapter 1: Introduction To C# 9
    What Is C#? 9
    Setting Up Your Development Environment 10
    Your First C# Program 12

Chapter 2: Variables and Types 23
    What Are Variables In C#? 23
    Data Types In C# 25
    Type Conversion (Also Known As Casting) 28
    Exercises 30
        Exercise Set 1 (Declaring and Using Variables) 30
        Exercise Set 2 (Data Types) 31
        Exercise Set 3 (Type Conversion) 32

Chapter 3: Control Flow 35
    Primer On Boolean Algebra 35
    Control Flow 36
    Conditional Statements (If/Else) 37
    Exercises 39
        Exercise Set 1 (If, Else, Else If) 39
    Loops (For, While, Do-While) 40
        Exercise Set 2 (Loops Using For, While, and Do-While)
       42
    Switch Statement 43
        Exercise Set 3 (Switch Statements) 44
    Break and Continue Statements 45
        Exercise Set 4 (Break and Continue) 46

Chapter 4: Functions 49
    Defining and Calling Functions 49
    Return Types and Parameters 50

    Exercise Set 1 (Functions) 51
    Local and Global Variables 53
        Exercise Set 2 (Local and Global Variables) 55

Chapter 5: Objects And Classes 57
    What are Objects And Classes? 57
    Creating A Class 59
    Instantiating And Using Objects From Classes 60
    Properties 62
    Methods 63
        Exercise Set 1 (Classes And Objects) 64
        Exercise Set 2 (Properties And Methods) 66

Chapter 6: Arrays And Collections 69
    Introduction To Arrays 69
    Working With Arrays 71
    Exercise Set 1 (Arrays) 72
    Collections (List, Dictionary, etc.) 73
        List 74
        Queue 75
        Stack 77
        Dictionary 78
    Exercise Set 2 (Collections) 79

Chapter 7: Exception Handling 81
    What Are Exceptions? 81
    Try-Catch-Finally Blocks 83
    Throwing Exceptions 85
    Exercises 87

Chapter 8: Final Project (Simple Console Game) 89
    Planning And Designing Your Game 89
    Implementing Your Game in C# 90
    Adding Polish and Finishing Touches 90

Chapter 9: More Projects 95

Practice Projects – Set 1 (Easy) 95
Practice Projects – Set 2 (Medium to Hard) 97

CHAPTER 1: INTRODUCTION TO C#

What you will learn in this chapter:
- What is C#?
- Setting up your development environment
- Your first C# program

WHAT IS C#?

C# is a modern, object-oriented programming language developed by Microsoft. It is designed to be simple, powerful, and easy to learn. C# is used to develop a wide variety of applications, including web, mobile, desktop, gaming, and IoT (Internet of Things) applications.

One of the key features of C# is its strong support for object-oriented programming, which is a programming paradigm that organizes code into "objects" that represent real-world entities and the actions that can be performed on them. This makes it easier to design, test, and maintain large software systems.

C# is also a statically-typed language, which means that variables must be declared with a specific type (such as int, string, or bool) and that type is checked at compile-time. This helps catch errors early on in the development process and makes the resulting code easier to understand and debug.

Overall, C# is a versatile and popular language that is well-suited for a wide range of programming tasks.

Disclaimer: This book is designed to teach you the core fundamentals of programming in C#. While the C# language has undergone many enhancements and changes with each new version, we will focus on the core language concepts that remain consistent across all versions of C#. This means that we will not cover language-specific features that have been introduced in later versions of C#, such as nullable reference types in C# 8.0 or records in C# 9.0. Instead, our focus will be on the core language constructs, data types, operators, and programming concepts that form the foundation of C# programming, and that will serve as a solid foundation for you to build upon as you continue to learn and grow as a C# developer.

SETTING UP YOUR DEVELOPMENT ENVIRONMENT

To set up your development environment for C#, you will need to install the following:

- a) A C# compiler: This is the software that will turn your C# code into an executable program. There are several C# compilers available, but the most popular one is called the .NET Core SDK, which Microsoft develops. Install the .NET Core SDK: In order to create and run a C# console application, you will need to

install the .NET Core SDK on your machine. You can download the latest version of the .NET Core SDK from the following link:
https://dotnet.microsoft.com/download

b) An Integrated Development Environment (IDE): This is a program that provides a convenient interface for writing, testing, and debugging your C# code. Some popular IDEs for C# include Visual Studio, Visual Studio Code, and MonoDevelop. You can download these IDEs from their respective websites. **For this course, we will use Visual Studio Code (VSCode)**, and you can download VSCode from the official Microsoft website. Here is the link:
https://code.visualstudio.com/download On this page, you will see a list of the available downloads for different operating systems. You can choose the appropriate version for your system and click the "Download" button to start the download process and install it.

Once you have installed a C# compiler and an IDE, you should be able to create a new C# project, write some code, and run it to see the results. It's also a good idea to set up a source control system (such as Git) to track changes to your code and collaborate with other developers.

You can find all the code in this book, and the solution to exercises at the following Github location:
https://github.com/qodecamp-com/CSharp_YourTicket

YOUR FIRST C# PROGRAM

Here is a simple "Hello, World!" program in C#:

```
using System;

namespace HelloWorld
{
    class Program
    {
        static void Main(string[] args)
        {
            Console.WriteLine("Hello, World!");
        }
    }
}
```

Here's an explanation of what's going on in this code:

using System;: This line includes the **System** namespace in the program. The **System** namespace contains many built-in types and methods that are used in the program.

namespace HelloWorld: A namespace is a container for a set of related classes. In this case, the **HelloWorld** namespace contains the **Program** class.

class Program: A class is a blueprint for an object. It defines the properties and behaviors of an object. In this case, the **Program** class contains the **Main** method, which is the entry point of the program.

static void Main(string[] args): The **Main** method is the entry point of the program. It is where the program begins execution. The **static** keyword indicates that the method belongs to the **Program** class, rather than an instance of the **Program** class. The **void** keyword indicates that the method does not return a value. The **string[] args** parameter is an array of strings that can be passed to the program when it is executed.

Console.WriteLine("Hello, World!");: This line writes the string "Hello, World!" to the console. The **Console** class is part of the **System** namespace, and the **WriteLine** method is a method of the **Console** class that writes a line of text to the console.

NOTE: If you are using a Macbook, you should be able to execute the same commands on the Mac "Terminal".

```
To open the Terminal on a Mac, follow these
steps:

1. Open the Finder and click "Applications"
   in the left-hand sidebar.
2. Scroll down until you see the "Utilities"
   folder and click it.
3. Look for the Terminal app and double-click
   it to launch it.

Alternatively, you can use the search
function to find the Terminal app. To do
this, click the magnifying glass icon in the
top right corner of the screen and type
"Terminal" into the search field. Then,
click on the Terminal app to launch it.

You can also use the Spotlight search
function to find the Terminal app. Press the
Command + Space keys on your keyboard to
open the Spotlight search, type "Terminal,"
and then press the Enter key to launch the
app.
```

Here are the steps to run this on your Windows computer:

- ***Run cmd***

To open the terminal in Windows, you can do the following:

1. Press the Windows key + R to open the "Run" dialog.
2. Type "cmd" into the "Run" dialog and press Enter. This will open the command prompt.

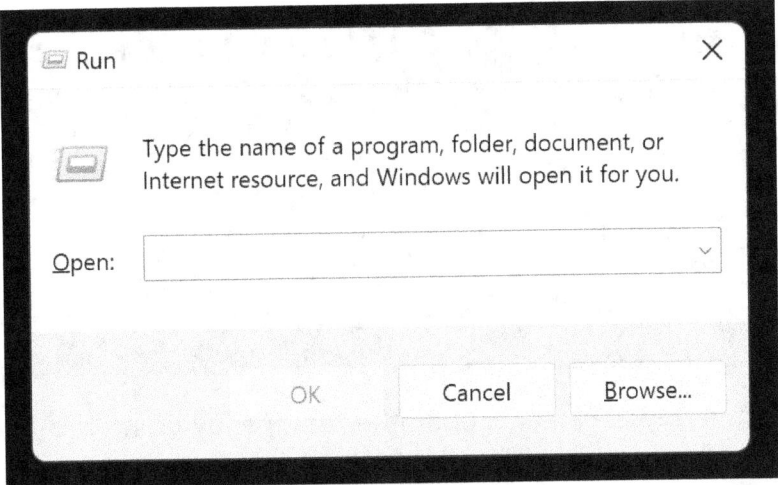

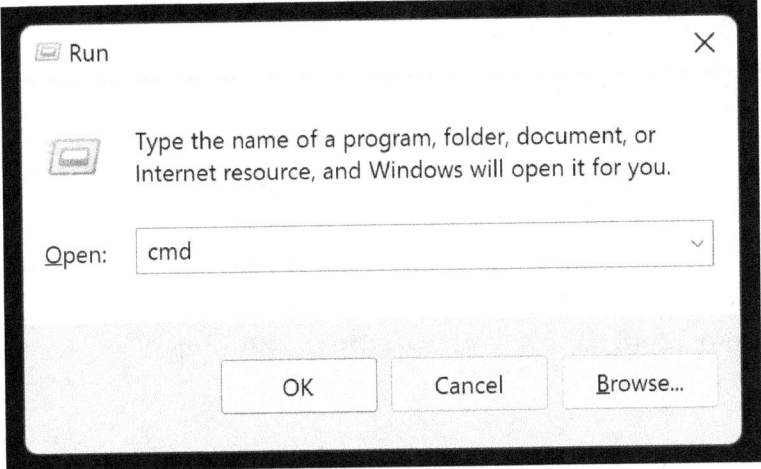

cmd.exe is the command-line interpreter for the Microsoft Windows operating system. It is used to execute commands from a command-line interface (CLI) or script. The CLI is a text-based interface for interacting with the operating system and running programs. It is also known as the command prompt or terminal. You can use cmd.exe to perform a wide range of tasks on your computer, such as managing files and directories, running programs, and modifying system settings.

```
Select C:\WINDOWS\system32\cmd.exe
Microsoft Windows [Version 10.0.22000.1335]
(c) Microsoft Corporation. All rights reserved.

C:\Users\andyv>
```

Alternatively, you can also open the terminal by doing the following:

1. Click the Start button.

2. Type "cmd" into the search bar and press Enter. This will open the command prompt.

You can also use the terminal by using the Windows Subsystem for Linux (WSL). To do this, you will need to install a Linux distribution from the Microsoft Store and then use the terminal that is provided with the distribution.

I like to keep all my code inside the Documents folder in a folder called code, so let's create the code folder

To create a new folder inside the "Documents" folder on the command line in Windows, you can use the "mkdir" (make directory) command.

Here is an example of how to use the "mkdir" command to create a new folder named "code" inside the "Documents" folder:

- Open the command prompt by pressing the Windows key + R, typing "cmd" into the "Run" dialog, and pressing Enter.

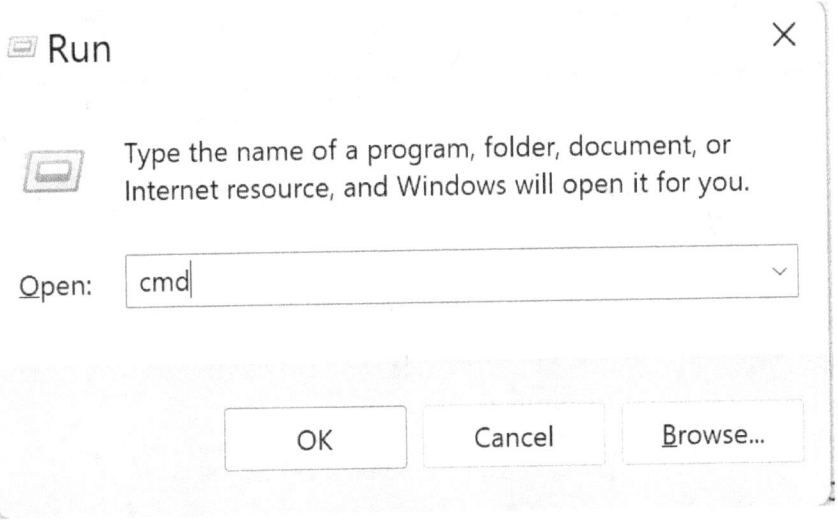

Running this command opens the Command Line Interface also known as the CLI. The default location is C:\users\[loggedInUserName]

- Navigate to the "Documents" folder

- To do this, you will need to use the cd (also known as Change Directory command)
- Type in cd Documents and hit Enter

```
cd Documents

OR provide the full Directory path like:
cd C:\Users\YourUsername\Documents\
```

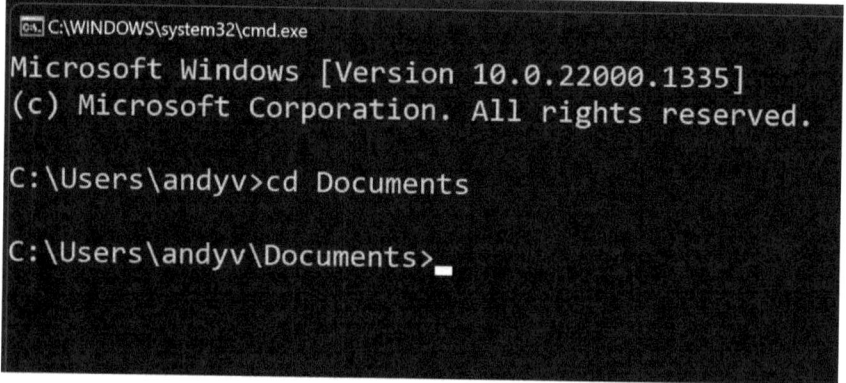

- Let's create the "code" folder where we will keep all our source code
    - To do this, you'll need to use the "mkdir" command also known as Make Directory command.
    - Type in mkdir code and hit Enter

```
mkdir code
```

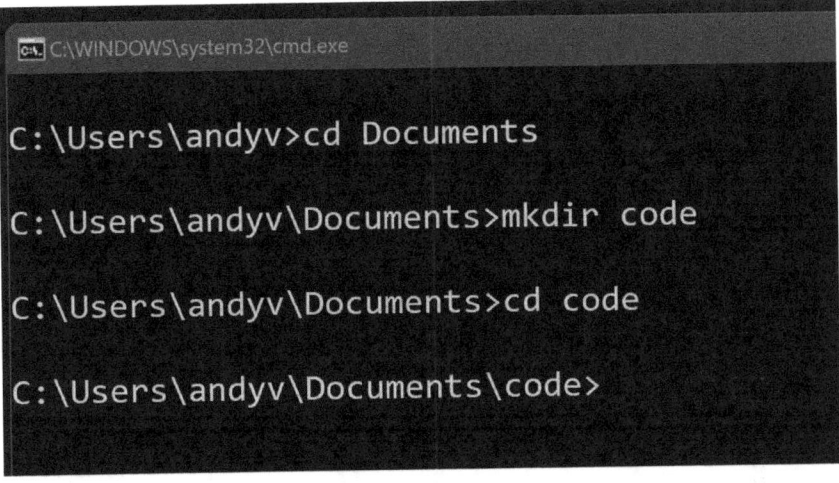

- Navigate to the newly created code folder/directory
    - To do this, you will once again use the cd command
    - Type in cd code and hit Enter

```
cd code
```

- The code folder is where we will create our Projects. Each new Project will have its own folder.
    - Let's create the HelloWorld folder and navigate to it.

```
C:\WINDOWS\system32\cmd.exe

C:\Users\andyv\Documents\code>mkdir HelloWorld

C:\Users\andyv\Documents\code>cd HelloWorld

C:\Users\andyv\Documents\code\HelloWorld>
```

- Create a new console application:
    - Step 1: Open a terminal window and navigate to the directory where you want to create your console application. (we are already in the correct folder, so you can skip this step)
    - Step 2: Run the following command to create a new console application:

```
dotnet new console --use-program-main
```

Note: we use the --use-program-main *flag to let the old-style program.cs to be created. The new style allows top-level statements without the need for a Main method. Let's skip this new approach for now.*

```
C:\WINDOWS\system32\cmd.exe

C:\Users\andyv\Documents\code>mkdir HelloWorld

C:\Users\andyv\Documents\code>cd HelloWorld

C:\Users\andyv\Documents\code\HelloWorld>dotnet new console --use-program-main
The template "Console App" was created successfully.

Processing post-creation actions...
Restoring C:\Users\andyv\Documents\code\HelloWorld\HelloWorld.csproj:
  Determining projects to restore...
  Restored C:\Users\andyv\Documents\code\HelloWorld\HelloWorld.csproj (in 55 ms).
Restore succeeded.


C:\Users\andyv\Documents\code\HelloWorld>
```

- Build the application: Navigate to the directory of the console application that you just created and run the following command to build the application:

```
dotnet build
```

```
C:\WINDOWS\system32\cmd.exe

C:\Users\andyv\Documents\code\HelloWorld>dotnet build
MSBuild version 17.4.0+18d5aef85 for .NET
  Determining projects to restore...
  All projects are up-to-date for restore.
  HelloWorld -> C:\Users\andyv\Documents\code\HelloWorld\bin\Debug\net7.0\HelloWorld.dll

Build succeeded.
    0 Warning(s)
    0 Error(s)

Time Elapsed 00:00:00.71

C:\Users\andyv\Documents\code\HelloWorld>
```

- Run the application: Once the application has been built, you can run it by using the following command:

```
dotnet run
```

```
C:\WINDOWS\system32\cmd.exe

C:\Users\andyv\Documents\code\HelloWorld>dotnet run
Hello, World!

C:\Users\andyv\Documents\code\HelloWorld>
```

Congrats! You just created and ran your first C# program. As you can see, "Hello, World!" gets printed to the console.

- Edit the code: Open the file named "Program.cs" in a text editor and add your C# code to the Main method. Save the file and then rebuild and run the application again to see the changes that you made.

```
For Mac users, if you run into issues
executing the dotnet command, please search
for the error shown on Google, and you
should be able to find the solution needed
to help you get unstuck.

For the remainder of the book, I will not be
provided step by step guidance for Mac
users. Once you get the environment
correctly setup, the dotnet commands you
issue on Windows and MacOS will be the same.
```

CHAPTER 2: VARIABLES AND TYPES

What you will learn in this chapter:
- Declaring and using variables
- Data types in C#
- Type conversion

WHAT ARE VARIABLES IN C#?

A variable in C# is like a little container that you can store a value in. You can think of it like a jar that you can put things in and take things out of. You can label your jars with a name, like "apples" or "oranges," and then you can put things in your jars and take them out whenever you want.

For example, let's say you have a jar labeled "apples" and you put 5 apples in it. The jar is like a variable and the label "apples" is like the name of the variable. The 5 apples are like the value that you're storing in the variable. Later on, you might want to take an apple out of the jar and eat it, or you might want to put another apple in the jar. You can do all of this using variables in C#.

There are different types of variables, just like there are different types of jars. For example, you might have a jar that's really big and can hold a lot of apples, or you might have a jar that's smaller and can only hold a few apples. In C#, you can use different types of variables for different types of values. For example, you might use a "string" variable to hold a bunch of letters (like a word or a sentence), or you might use a "double" variable to hold a number with a decimal point (like 3.14).

In C# (and in programming in general), a variable is a named storage location in a program's memory that holds a value. Variables store data that can be manipulated or used in various parts of the program.

In C#, variables must be declared before they can be used. You need to specify the type of data the variable will hold (such as int, string, or bool) and give it a unique name. For example:

```
int age;
string name;
bool isValid;
```

Once a variable is declared, you can assign a value using the assignment operator (=). For example:

```
age = 30;
name = "John";
isValid = true;
```

You can then use the variable in your code by referencing its name. For example:

```
Console.WriteLine("Your name is " + name + " and you are " + age + " years old.");
```

It's important to note that the value of a variable can change over time, as it can be reassigned a new value at any point in the program.

DATA TYPES IN C#

In C#, a data type is a classification of types of data that determines the possible values for that type, the operations that can be performed on it, and the way it is stored in the computer's memory.

Here are the most common data types in C#:

- Numeric data types: These include integers (such as int and long), floating-point numbers (such as float and double), and decimal numbers (decimal).
- Boolean data type: This data type represents a true or false value. It is represented by the bool keyword.
- Character data type: This data type represents a single character, such as a letter or symbol. It is represented by the char keyword.
- String data type: This data type represents a sequence of characters, such as a word or a phrase. It is represented by the string keyword.
- Object data type: This data type represents any object in C#. It is represented by the object keyword.

There are also several other data types in C#, such as arrays, enums, and structs.

It's important to choose the appropriate data type for your variables, as it can affect the performance and accuracy of your program. For example, using a float data type to store a large integer value might result in loss of precision, as float values have a limited number of decimal places.

Here is a list of the common data types in C# and their applications:

- int (integer): This data type represents a whole number. It can store values from -2147483648 to 2147483647. It is commonly used to store counts, ages, and other values that do not have a fractional component.
- long (long integer): This data type is similar to int, but it can store larger values. It can store values from -9223372036854775808 to 9223372036854775807.
- float (floating-point): This data type represents a number with a fractional component. It is accurate to 7 decimal places and is commonly used to store values that require a high degree of precision, such as scientific or financial data.
- double (double-precision floating-point): This data type is similar to float, but it is more accurate, with a precision of 15-16 decimal places. It is often used for large and complex calculations.
- decimal (decimal number): This data type represents a number with a fractional component, similar to float and double. However, it is more accurate and is commonly used for financial applications requiring high precision.

- bool (boolean): This data type represents a true or false value. It is commonly used for flags and conditions in a program.
- char (character): This data type represents a single character, such as a letter or symbol. It is stored as a single Unicode character.
- string (string): This data type represents a sequence of characters, such as a word or a phrase. It is stored as an array of char values.
- object (object): This data type represents any object in C#. It is a reference type that can store any value, including the values of other data types.

In C#, the default value for a common data type is the value that is assigned to a variable of that type when it is declared but not initialized.

Here is a list of the default values for some common data types in C#:

Data type	Default value
bool	false
byte	0
char	'\0'
decimal	0.0m
double	0.0d
float	0.0f
int	0
long	0L
sbyte	0
short	0

Data type	Default value
uint	0u
ulong	0ul
ushort	0

Note that reference types (such as strings and arrays) have a default value of null, which means that they don't refer to any object.

It's important to keep in mind that these are the default values for variables that are declared but **not** initialized. If you initialize a variable with a specific value, that value will be assigned to the variable, regardless of its data type.

For example:
```
int x = 10;   // the value of x is 10, not 0
string name = "Alice";   // the value of name is "Alice", not null
```

TYPE CONVERSION (ALSO KNOWN AS CASTING)

In C#, type conversion is the process of converting a value from one data type to another. This is also known as type casting.

There are two types of type conversion in C#: implicit and explicit.

- Implicit type conversion: This type of conversion is automatically performed by the C# compiler when the value being converted is compatible with the target

data type. For example, you can assign an int value to a long variable without specifying any type conversion, because an int value is compatible with a long variable.
- Explicit type conversion: This type of conversion requires you to specify the target data type using a type casting operator. For example, you can use the (long) operator to explicitly convert an int value to a long value. This is necessary when the value being converted is not compatible with the target data type, as it might result in data loss.

Here is an example of implicit type conversion in C#:

```
int x = 10; long y = x; // Implicit type conversion from int to long
```

And here is an example of explicit type conversion:

```
// Explicit type conversion from long to int
long x = 10; int y = (int)x;
```

It's important to be careful when performing explicit type conversions, as they can result in data loss if the target data type is not large enough to hold the converted value.

Here is an example of data loss that can occur with type conversion in C#:

```
int a = 2000000;
float b = a;
Console.WriteLine(b);   // Output: 2000000
int c = (int)b;
Console.WriteLine(c);   // Output: 1999999
```

In this example, the value of a is converted from an **int** to a **float**, which works fine because an **int** can be represented exactly as a float. However, when the value of b is then converted back to an **int** and stored in c, the value is not the same as the original value of a. This is because the value of b is not exactly representable as an **int**, so it is rounded down to the nearest representable value. This results in a loss of data.

EXERCISES

EXERCISE SET 1 (DECLARING AND USING VARIABLES)

1. Declare a string variable called "name" and assign it your own name. Then, print out the value of the variable to the console.
2. Declare an integer variable called "age" and assign it your own age. Then, print out the value of the variable to the console.
3. Declare a double variable called "temperature" and assign it a value of 98.6. Then, print out the value of the variable to the console.
4. Declare a boolean variable called "isRaining" and assign it a value of true or false based on the current weather. Then, print out the value of the variable to the console.

5. Declare a char variable called "initial" and assign it the first letter of your name. Then, print out the value of the variable to the console.
6. Declare a variable of a custom type that you create yourself. For example, you could create a "Person" type with variables for "name" and "age". Then, create an instance of your custom type and assign values to its variables. Finally, print out the values of the variables to the console.

EXERCISE SET 2 (DATA TYPES)

1. Declare a variable of each data type: bool, char, int, double, string. Initialize each variable with a value of your choosing, then print out the value and type of each variable to the console.
2. Write a program that prompts the user to enter a number. Then, store the number in a variable of the appropriate data type. Finally, print out the number on the console.

   HINT: To read input from the console in C#, you can use the Console.ReadLine method. This method reads a line of text from the console, which you can then assign to a string variable.

   For example:

```
string input;
input = Console.ReadLine();
```

This will read a line of text from the console and store it in the input variable.

You can also use the Console.Read method to read a single character from the console. This method returns an integer representing the ASCII code of the character that was read.

For example:
```
int input;
input = Console.Read();
```

This will read a single character from the console and store its ASCII code in the input variable.

3. Write a program that prompts the user to enter their name and age. Store the name in a string variable and the age in an int variable. Then, print out a message to the console that says "Hello, [name]! You are [age] years old."
4. Write a program that declares a double variable called "diameter" and assigns it a value of 12.5. Then, declare a second variable called "radius" and assign it the value of the diameter divided by 2. Finally, print out the value of the radius to the console.

EXERCISE SET 3 (TYPE CONVERSION)

1. Declare a double variable and assign it a value of 3.5. Then, declare an int variable and assign it the value of the double variable, using type conversion. Finally, print out the value of the int variable to the console.

2. Declare a string variable and assign it a value of "4". Then, declare an int variable and assign it the value of the string variable, using type conversion. Finally, print out the value of the int variable to the console.
3. Declare a bool variable and assign it a value of true. Then, declare an int variable and assign it the value of the bool variable, using type conversion. Finally, print out the value of the int variable to the console.
4. Declare an int variable and assign it a value of 10. Then, declare a double variable and assign it the value of the int variable, using type conversion. Finally, print out the value of the double variable to the console.
5. Write a program that prompts the user to enter a number in pounds (lbs). Then, convert the entered value to kilograms (kgs) and print out the result to the console. [Hint: 1 kilogram (kg) = 2.2 pounds/lbs]

CHAPTER 3: CONTROL FLOW

What you will learn in this chapter:
- Primer on Boolean Algebra
- Conditional statements (if/else)
- Loops (for, while, do-while)
- Switch statements

PRIMER ON BOOLEAN ALGEBRA

Boolean algebra is a mathematical system for representing and manipulating logical expressions. In C#, boolean algebra can be used in a number of ways, including controlling the flow of programs through the use of conditional statements and performing logical operations on variables.

Here are the basic logical operations in C#:

- **&&**: represents the logical AND operation. It returns **true** if both operands are **true**, and **false** otherwise.

- **||**: represents the logical OR operation. It returns **true** if either of the operands is **true**, and **false** otherwise.

- **!**: represents the logical NOT operation. It negates a boolean value, returning **true** if the operand is **false**, and **false** if the operand is **true**.

Here is an example of how these operators can be used in C#:

```
bool a = true;
bool b = false;

bool c = a && b;   // c is false
bool d = a || b;   // d is true
bool e = !a;       // e is false
```

Boolean algebra also includes several compound logical operators that can be used to create more complex expressions. These include:

- **&**: represents the bitwise AND operation. It performs a logical AND operation on each bit of its operands.
- **|**: represents the bitwise OR operation. It performs a logical OR operation on each bit of its operands.
- **^**: represents the bitwise XOR (exclusive OR) operation. It performs a logical XOR operation on each bit of its operands.

Here is an example of how these operators can be used in C#:

```
int x = 5;   // binary representation: 0101
int y = 3;   // binary representation: 0011

int z = x & y;   // z is 1 (binary representation: 0001)
int w = x | y;   // w is 7 (binary representation: 0111)
int u = x ^ y;   // u is 6 (binary representation: 0110)
```

CONTROL FLOW

Control flow refers to the order in which the instructions in a program are executed. In C#, control flow is implemented using statements that allow you to specify the order in which the statements in your code are executed. Some of the control flow statements in C# include:

1. **if** statements, which allow you to execute a block of code only if a certain condition is true

2. **for** loops, which allow you to repeat a block of code a certain number of times

3. **while** loops, which allow you to repeat a block of code while a certain condition is true

4. **switch** statements, which allow you to execute a different block of code depending on the value of an expression.

There are several other control flow statements in C# as well, each of which serves a specific purpose and can be used to implement different types of control flow in your code.

CONDITIONAL STATEMENTS (IF/ELSE)

if statements in C# allow you to execute a block of code only if a certain condition is true. Here's the basic syntax for an if statement:

```
if (condition)
{
    // code to execute if condition is true
}
```

You can also include an **else** clause to specify a block of code to be executed if the condition is false:

```
if (condition)
{
    // code to execute if condition is true
}
else
{
    // code to execute if condition is false
```

```
}
```

You can also include multiple **else if** clauses to specify additional conditions to be tested:

```
if (condition1)
{
    // code to execute if condition1 is true
}
else if (condition2)
{
    // code to execute if condition1 is false and condition2 is true
}
else
{
    // code to execute if both condition1 and condition2 are false
}
```

Here's an example of an **if** statement that checks whether a variable **x** is greater than 10:

```
int x = 15;

if (x > 10)
{
    Console.WriteLine("x is greater than 10");
}
```

This **if** statement would output "x is greater than 10" to the console, because the condition **x > 10** is true.

Here are a few examples that include **else** and **else if** clauses:

```
int x = 15;

if (x > 20)
{
    Console.WriteLine("x is greater than 20");
}
else if (x > 10)
{
    Console.WriteLine("x is greater than 10 but less than 20");
}
else
{
    Console.WriteLine("x is less than 10");
```

```
}
```

This if statement would output "x is greater than 10 but not greater than 20" to the console, because the condition x > 20 is false and the condition x > 10 is true.

Here's another example that checks whether a string is equal to "hello":

```
string str = "hello";
if (str == "hello")
{
    Console.WriteLine("str is equal to 'hello'");
}
else if (str == "world")
{
    Console.WriteLine("str is equal to 'world'");
}
else
{
    Console.WriteLine("str is not equal to 'hello' or 'world'");
}
```

This if statement would output "str is equal to 'hello'" to the console, because the condition str == "hello" is true.

EXERCISES

EXERCISE SET 1 (IF, ELSE, ELSE IF)

Here are a few exercises to practice using if statements in C#:

1. Write a program that asks the user to enter a number, and then displays a message indicating whether the number is positive, negative, or zero.

2. Write a program that asks the user to enter a letter of the alphabet, and then displays a message indicating whether the letter is a vowel or a consonant.

3. Write a program that asks the user to enter their age, and then displays a message indicating whether the user is an adult (age 18 or older), a teenager (age 13 to 17), or a child (age 12 or younger).

4. Write a program that asks the user to enter a temperature in degrees Celsius, and then displays the equivalent temperature in degrees Fahrenheit. HINT: The formula to convert Celsius to Fahrenheit is - F = C * 9/5 + 32

5. Write a program that asks the user to enter a number, and then displays a message indicating whether the number is odd or even.

LOOPS (FOR, WHILE, DO-WHILE)

In C#, there are three types of loops: for loops, while loops, and do-while loops.

1. **for** loops are used to execute a block of code a specific number of times. The syntax for a for loop is:

```
for (initialization; condition; iteration)
{
    // code to be executed
}
```

The initialization clause is executed once, before the loop starts. The condition is checked before each iteration of the loop. If the condition is true, the loop continues to execute. If the condition is false, the loop terminates. The iteration clause is executed after each iteration of the loop.

Here's an example of a **for** loop that counts from 1 to 10:

```
for (int i = 1; i <= 10; i++)
{
    Console.WriteLine(i);
}
```

This loop would output the numbers 1 through 10 to the console.

2. **while** loops are used to execute a block of code as long as a certain condition is true. The syntax for a **while** loop is:

```
while (condition)
{
    // code to be executed
}
```

The condition is checked before each iteration of the loop. If the condition is true, the loop continues to execute. If the condition is false, the loop terminates.

Here's an example of a **while** loop that counts from 1 to 10:

```
int i = 1;
while (i <= 10)
{
    Console.WriteLine(i);
    i++;
}
```

This loop would output the numbers 1 through 10 to the console.

3. **do-while** loops are similar to **while** loops, but the condition is checked after each iteration of the loop instead of before. The syntax for a **do-while** loop is:

```
do
{
    // code to be executed
```

```
}
while (condition);
```

The code in the do loop is executed at least once, because the condition is checked after the first iteration. If the condition is true, the loop continues to execute. If the condition is false, the loop terminates.

Here's an example of a **do-while** loop that counts from 1 to 10:

```
int i = 1;
do
{
    Console.WriteLine(i);
    i++;
} while (i <= 10);
```

This loop would also output the numbers 1 through 10 to the console.

EXERCISE SET 2 (LOOPS USING FOR, WHILE, AND DO-WHILE)

Here are a few exercises to practice using loops in C#:

1. Write a program that uses a for loop to count from 1 to 10 and display the numbers to the console.

2. Write a program that uses a while loop to count from 1 to 10 and display the numbers to the console.

3. Write a program that uses a do-while loop to count from 1 to 10 and display the numbers to the console.

4. Write a program that asks the user to enter a number, and then uses a for loop to count from 1 to that number and display the numbers to the console.

5. Write a program that asks the user to enter a number, and then uses a while loop to count from 1 to that number and display the numbers to the console.

6. Write a program that asks the user to enter a number, and then uses a do-while loop to count from 1 to that number and display the numbers to the console.

SWITCH STATEMENT

switch statements in C# allow you to execute a block of code based on the value of an expression. The syntax for a **switch** statement is:

```
switch (expression)
{
    case value1:
        // code to execute if expression == value1
        break;
    case value2:
        // code to execute if expression == value2
        break;
    ... //add more case statements as needed
    default:
        // code to execute if expression does not match any of the case values
        break;
}
```

The expression is evaluated, and the value is compared to the values in each **case** clause. If a match is found, the code in the corresponding **case** clause is executed. If no match is found, the code in the **default** clause is executed. The **break** statement is used to exit the **switch** statement and prevent the code in the following **case** clauses from being executed.

Here's an example of a **switch** statement that checks the value of a variable **x** and displays a message based on its value:

```
int x = 2;
```

```
switch (x)
{
    case 1:
        Console.WriteLine("x is 1");
        break;
    case 2:
        Console.WriteLine("x is 2");
        break;
    case 3:
        Console.WriteLine("x is 3");
        break;
    default:
        Console.WriteLine("x is not 1, 2, or 3");
        break;
}
```

This **switch** statement would output "x is 2" to the console, because the value of **x** is 2.

Here's a practical application of a **switch** statement that accepts user input and runs indefinitely inside a **while** loop, with an explicit case that exits the loop:

```
boolean flag = true;

while (flag)
{
    Console.WriteLine("Enter a command (exit to quit):");
    string command = Console.ReadLine();

    switch (command)
    {
        case "exit":
            Console.WriteLine("Exiting loop...");
//set the flag to false so it fails the test on the while loop
            flag = false;
            return;
        case "print":
            Console.WriteLine("Enter a message to print:");
            string message = Console.ReadLine();
            Console.WriteLine(message);
            break;
        default:
            Console.WriteLine("Invalid command.");
            break;
    }
}
```

EXERCISE SET 3 (SWITCH STATEMENTS)

Here are a few exercises to practice using **switch** statements in C#:

1. Write a program that declares a char variable called "grade" and assigns it a letter grade (A, B, C, D, or F). Then, use a switch statement to print out a message to the console based on the value of the grade. For example, if the grade is an A, the message should say "Excellent job!"

2. Write a program that asks the user to enter a letter of the alphabet, and then displays a message indicating whether the letter is a vowel or a consonant.

3. Write a program that asks the user to enter a number, and then displays a message indicating whether the number is positive, negative, or zero.

4. Write a program that asks the user to enter a month of the year (as a number), and then displays the number of days in that month.

5. Write a program that asks the user to enter a day of the week, and then displays a message indicating whether it is a weekday or a weekend.

6. Write a program that asks the user to enter a year, and then displays a message indicating whether the year is a leap year or not.

BREAK AND CONTINUE STATEMENTS

break statements in C# are used to exit a loop or a switch statement. When a **break** statement is encountered inside a loop, the loop is immediately terminated and control is transferred to the statement following the loop.

Here's an example of a **break** statement inside a **for** loop:

```
for (int i = 1; i <= 10; i++)
{
    if (i == 5)
    {
        break;
    }
    Console.WriteLine(i);
}
```

This loop would output the numbers 1 through 4 to the console, because the **break** statement is encountered when **i** is 5 and the loop is terminated.

continue statements in C# are used to skip the remaining statements in the current iteration of a loop and immediately start the next iteration.

Here's an example of a **continue** statement inside a **for** loop:

```
for (int i = 1; i <= 10; i++)
{
    if (i % 2 == 0)
    {
        continue;
    }
    Console.WriteLine(i);
}
```

This loop would output the numbers 1, 3, 5, 7, and 9 to the console, because the **continue** statement is encountered when **i** is even and the remaining statements in the current iteration are skipped.

EXERCISE SET 4 (BREAK AND CONTINUE)

Here are a few exercises to practice using **break** and **continue** statements in C#:

1. Write a program that uses a for loop to count from 1 to 10, but only displays the odd numbers.

2. Write a program that uses a while loop to count from 1 to 10, but only displays the even numbers.

3. Write a program that uses a do-while loop to count from 1 to 10, but displays the numbers in reverse order.

4. Write a program that asks the user to enter a number, and then uses a for loop to count from 1 to that number, but only displays the numbers that are divisible by 3.

5. Write a program that asks the user to enter a number, and then uses a while loop to count from 1 to that number, but only displays the numbers that are not divisible by 4.

CHAPTER 4: FUNCTIONS

What you will learn in this chapter:
- Defining and calling functions
- Return types and parameters
- Global and Local Variables

DEFINING AND CALLING FUNCTIONS

In C#, functions are blocks of code that perform a specific task and can be called from other parts of your code. Defining a function involves specifying its name, its return type (if any), and its parameters (if any). Calling a function involves specifying its name and providing any required parameters.

Here's an example of a function in C# that calculates the area of a rectangle:

```
int CalculateRectangleArea(int length, int width)
{
    int area = length * width;
    return area;
}
```

This function, named **CalculateRectangleArea**, takes two integers as parameters (**length** and **width**) and returns an integer (the area of the rectangle).

To call this function from another part of your code, you would write:

```
int length = 10;
int width = 5;
int rectangleArea = CalculateRectangleArea(length, width);
```

This would call the **CalculateRectangleArea** function, passing the values **length** and **width** as arguments. The function would execute and return the value 50, which would be assigned to the **rectangleArea** variable.

RETURN TYPES AND PARAMETERS

In C#, a function's return type is the data type of the value that the function returns to the calling code. A function can have no return type (in which case it is a void function), or it can have a specific return type such as int, double, string, etc.

Here's an example of a function with a return type in C#:

```
int CalculateRectangleArea(int length, int width)
{
    int area = length * width;
    return area;
}
```

This function, named **CalculateRectangleArea**, has a return type of **int** and returns the product of the **length** and **width** parameters as an integer.

Parameters are the values that a function uses as input. A function can have no parameters, or it can have one or more parameters of a specific data type. When defining a function, the parameters are listed in the function signature in the order in which they are expected to be passed. When calling a function, the arguments are passed in the same order as the parameters.

Here's an example of a function with parameters in C#:

```
int CalculateRectangleArea(int length, int width)
{
    int area = length * width;
    return area;
}

int length = 10;
int width = 5;
int rectangleArea = CalculateRectangleArea(length, width);
```

This function, named **CalculateRectangleArea**, has two parameters: **length** and **width**, both of type **int**. When the function is called, the values **length** and **width** are passed as arguments. The function calculates the area of the rectangle by multiplying the **length** and **width** parameters and returns the result as an **int**.

EXERCISE SET 1 (FUNCTIONS)

Here are a few exercises to practice creating and calling functions in C#:

1. Write a function that takes two integers as parameters and returns the sum of the two numbers. Call the function from your main program and display the result.

2. Write a function that takes a string as a parameter and returns the string with all vowels removed. Call the function from your main program and display the result.

3. Write a function that takes three integers as parameters and returns the largest of the three

numbers. Call the function from your main program and display the result.

4. Write a function that takes a double as a parameter and returns the square root of the number. Call the function from your main program and display the result.

HINT: In C#, you can use the `Math.Sqrt` method to calculate the square root of a number. This method returns the square root of its input as a double-precision floating-point number.

Here is an example of how to use the `Math.Sqrt` method:

```
double x = 4.0;
double y = Math.Sqrt(x);   // y will be 2.0
```

The `Math.Sqrt` method can be used to calculate the square root of any positive number. If you pass a negative number to this method, it will throw an exception.

You can also use the `Math.Pow` method to calculate the square root of a number by raising it to the power of 0.5. This method returns the result of the specified number raised to the specified power.

Here is an example of how to use the `Math.Pow` method to calculate the square root of a number:

```
double x = 4.0;
double y = Math.Pow(x, 0.5);   // y will be 2.0
```

Write a function that takes a string as a parameter and returns the string in all uppercase. Call the function from your main program and display the result.

HINT: Here is an example of how to use the `ToUpper` method. Strings have an inbuilt method called **ToUpper** that you can call on the string object.

```
string input = "hello world";
string output = input.ToUpper();   // output will be "HELLO WORLD"
```

LOCAL AND GLOBAL VARIABLES

In C#, a variable is a location in memory where you can store a value of a specific type. There are two types of variables in C#: local variables and global variables.

Local variables are variables that are defined within a function and are only accessible within that function. Local variables are created when the function is called and are destroyed when the function returns. Local variables have function scope, meaning that they are only visible within the function in which they are defined.

Here's an example of a local variable in C#:

```
void PrintNumber(int number)
{
    int localVariable = number * 2;
    Console.WriteLine(localVariable);
}
```

In this example, the variable **localVariable** is a local variable that is defined within the **PrintNumber** function. It is assigned the value of the **number** parameter multiplied by 2, and then printed to the console.

Global variables are variables that are defined outside of any function and are accessible from any function in your code. Global variables have global scope, meaning that they are visible to all functions in your code.

Here's an example of a global variable in C#:

```
int globalVariable = 10;
void PrintNumber(int number)
{
    Console.WriteLine(globalVariable + number);
}
```

Important note on Global Variables: It is generally recommended to avoid using global variables in your code because they can make your code harder to read and maintain.

One reason to avoid using global variables is that they can make it more difficult to understand how your code works. Global variables can be accessed and modified from any function, which can make it harder to trace the flow of your code and understand how it is working.

Another reason to avoid using global variables is that they can lead to conflicts if multiple functions try to access or modify the same global variable at the same time. This can result in unexpected behavior and can be difficult to debug. You might be wondering how multiple functions can modify a single global variable. We'll learn more about it in classes and properties.

It is generally a better practice to use local variables, which are only visible within a specific function and do not have the potential to cause conflicts or confusion with other parts of your code.

EXERCISE SET 2 (LOCAL AND GLOBAL VARIABLES)

Here are some exercises to practice local and global variables in C#:

1. Create a program that calculates the area of a circle. The radius of the circle should be a local variable in the CalculateArea() method. The value of Pi should be a global constant.

2. Create a program that calculates the factorial of a number. The number should be a local variable in the CalculateFactorial() method. The factorial should be calculated using a global variable that stores the intermediate result as the calculation progresses.

3. Create a program that calculates the average of a list of numbers. The list of numbers should be a global variable. The average should be calculated in a local variable in the CalculateAverage() method.

4. Create a program that calculates the sum of the elements in a 2D array. The array should be a global variable. The sum should be calculated in a local variable in the CalculateSum() method.

HINT: You can skip this exercise for now, and return to it once you've learned about arrays in a later chapter.

5. Create a program that calculates the maximum value in a list of numbers. The list of numbers should be a global variable. The maximum value should be calculated in a local variable in the FindMaximum() method.

CHAPTER 5: OBJECTS AND CLASSES

What you will learn in this chapter:

- What are objects and classes?
- Creating a class
- Instantiating an object
- Accessing object properties and methods

WHAT ARE OBJECTS AND CLASSES?

In C#, an object is an instance of a class. A class is a blueprint or template for creating objects. It defines the properties and behaviors that the objects of the class will have.

For example, consider the following class in C#:

```
class Student
{
    public string Name { get; set; }
    public int Age { get; set; }
    public string Course { get; set; }

    public void AttendClass()
    {
        Console.WriteLine("{0} is attending class.", Name);
    }

    public void SubmitAssignment()
    {
        Console.WriteLine("{0} has submitted the assignment.", Name);
    }
}
```

This **Student** class has three properties: **Name**, **Age**, and **Course**. It also has two methods: **AttendClass** and **SubmitAssignment**.

To create an object of the **Student** class, you would write:

```
Student student1 = new Student();
```

You can then access the object's properties and methods using the dot notation:

```
student1.Name = "John";
student1.Age = 20;
student1.Course = "Computer Science";

student1.AttendClass();
student1.SubmitAssignment();
```

The output of this code would be:

```
John is attending class.
John has submitted the assignment.
```

You can also create multiple objects of the same class:

```
Student student2 = new Student();
student2.Name = "Jane";
student2.Age = 21;
student2.Course = "Mathematics";

Student student3 = new Student();
student3.Name = "Bob";
student3.Age = 22;
student3.Course = "Physics";
```

Each object has its own set of properties and behaviors, but they are all of the same class and share the same blueprint.

CREATING A CLASS

In C#, a class is a blueprint or template for creating objects. It defines the properties and behaviors that the objects of the class will have.

To create a class in C#, use the **class** keyword followed by the name of the class. The class definition should be placed inside a pair of curly braces. For example:

```
class Student
{
    // class definition goes here
}
```

Inside the class definition, you can define properties, fields, and methods.

Properties are used to store and retrieve data for an object. They have a getter and a setter, which allow you to read and write the property value. For example:

```
class Student
{
    public string Name { get; set; }
    public int Age { get; set; }
    public string Course { get; set; }
}
```

Fields are used to store data for an object, but they do not have a getter or setter. They are usually marked as **private** to prevent external code from directly accessing or modifying the field value. For example:

```
class Student
{
    private int studentId;
    public int Age { get; set; }
    public string Course { get; set; }
}
```

Methods are used to represent the behaviors of an object. They are defined using the **void** keyword followed by the name of the method. For example:

```
class Student
{
    public void AttendClass()
    {
        Console.WriteLine("Attending class...");
    }

    public void SubmitAssignment()
    {
        Console.WriteLine("Submitting assignment...");
    }
}
```

You can also define constructors for a class, which are special methods that are called when an object of the class is created. For example:

```
class Student
{
    public string Name { get; set; }
    public int Age { get; set; }
    public string Course { get; set; }

    public Student(string name, int age, string course)
    {
        Name = name;
        Age = age;
        Course = course;
    }
}
```

INSTANTIATING AND USING OBJECTS FROM CLASSES

To create an object of a class, you use the new keyword followed by the name of the class and a set of parentheses. For example:

```
Student student1 = new Student("John", 20, "Computer Science");
```

Here are some examples of creating objects from the Student class using the constructor method defined in the class:

```
Student student1 = new Student("John", 20, "Computer Science");
Student student2 = new Student("Jane", 21, "Mathematics");
Student student3 = new Student("Bob", 22, "Physics");
```

Each object has its own set of properties and behaviors, but they are all of the same class and share the same blueprint.

You can then access the object's properties and methods using the dot notation:

```
student1.Name = "John";
student1.Age = 20;
student1.Course = "Computer Science";

student1.AttendClass();
student1.SubmitAssignment();
```

The output of this code would be:

```
Attending class...
Submitting assignment...
```

You can also create an object of the Student class using the default constructor, which does not have any parameters:

```
Student student4 = new Student();
```

In this case, you would need to set the object's properties separately:

```
student4.Name = "Alice";
student4.Age = 23;
student4.Course = "Biology";
student4.AttendClass();
student4.SubmitAssignment();
```

PROPERTIES

In C#, properties are used to store and retrieve data for an object. They are defined in a class and have a getter and a setter, which allow you to read and write the property value.

Properties are defined using the **public** keyword followed by the type of the property and the name of the property. The getter and setter are defined using the **get** and **set** keywords, respectively. For example:

```
class Student
{
    public string Name { get; set; }
    public int Age { get; set; }
    public string Course { get; set; }
}
```

In this example, the **Student** class has three properties: **Name**, **Age**, and **Course**.

To access the property value, you use the dot notation:

```
Student student1 = new Student();
student1.Name = "John";
student1.Age = 20;
student1.Course = "Computer Science";

string name = student1.Name;
int age = student1.Age;
string course = student1.Course;
```

You can also define custom getters and setters for a property to specify how the property value is retrieved and set. For example:

```
class Student
```

```
{
    private string name;
    public string Name
    {
        get { return name; }
        set { name = value; }
    }

    public int Age { get; set; }
    public string Course { get; set; }
}
```

In this example, the **Name** property has a custom getter and setter that use a private field **name** to store the property value.

METHODS

In C#, methods are used to represent the behaviors of an object. They are defined in a class and are called using the dot notation.

To define a method in C#, use the **void** keyword followed by the name of the method and a set of parentheses. For example:

```
class Student
{
    public void AttendClass()
    {
        Console.WriteLine("Attending class...");
    }

    public void SubmitAssignment()
    {
        Console.WriteLine("Submitting assignment...");
    }
}
```

In this example, the **Student** class has two methods: **AttendClass** and **SubmitAssignment**.

To access a method, you use the dot notation followed by the name of the method and a set of parentheses:

```
Student student1 = new Student();
student1.AttendClass();
student1.SubmitAssignment();
```

You can also pass parameters to a method to customize its behavior. For example:

```
class Student
{
    public void AttendClass(string course)
    {
        Console.WriteLine("Attending {0} class...", course);
    }

    public void SubmitAssignment(string assignmentName)
    {
        Console.WriteLine("Submitting {0} assignment...", assignmentName);
    }
}
```

In this example, the **AttendClass** method takes a **course** parameter, and the **SubmitAssignment** method takes an **assignmentName** parameter. To call these methods, you would pass the required parameters in the parentheses:

```
Student student1 = new Student();
student1.AttendClass("Computer Science");
student1.SubmitAssignment("Math");
```

The output of this code would be:

```
Attending Computer Science class...
Submitting Math assignment...
```

EXERCISE SET 1 (CLASSES AND OBJECTS)

Here are some exercises to practice creating classes and objects in C#:

1. Create a Person class with properties for Name, Age, and Gender. Add a method called Introduce() that prints a greeting including the person's name. Create an object of the Person class and call the Introduce() method.

2. Create a Car class with properties for Make, Model, and Year. Add a method called StartEngine() that prints a message saying "Engine starting...". Create an object of the Car class and call the StartEngine() method.

3. Create a BankAccount class with properties for AccountNumber, Balance, and Owner. Add a method called Deposit() that allows the user to add money to the account. Add a method called Withdraw() that allows the user to withdraw money from the account. Create an object of the BankAccount class and call the Deposit() and Withdraw() methods to see if they work correctly.

4. Create a Book class with properties for Title, Author, and NumberOfPages. Add a method called Read() that takes a number of pages as a parameter and prints a message saying "Reading {number} pages...". Create an object of the Book class and call the Read() method.

5. Create a Television class with properties for Brand, Model, and Volume. Add a method called TurnOn() that prints a message saying "TV turning on...". Add a method called TurnOff() that prints a message saying "TV turning off...". Create an object of the Television class and call the TurnOn() and TurnOff() methods.

EXERCISE SET 2 (PROPERTIES AND METHODS)

Here are some exercises to practice properties and methods in C#:

1. Create a Rectangle class with properties for Length and Width. Add a method called GetArea() that calculates and returns the area of the rectangle. Create an object of the Rectangle class and call the GetArea() method to see if it works correctly.

2. Create a Circle class with a property for Radius. Add a method called GetCircumference() that calculates and returns the circumference of the circle. Add a method called GetArea() that calculates and returns the area of the circle. Create an object of the Circle class and call the GetCircumference() and GetArea() methods to see if they work correctly.

3. Write a method IsEven that takes in an integer and returns a boolean indicating whether the number is even.

4. Write a property FullName for a student class that gets and sets the student's first and last name. HINT:

Combine the first and last names in the Property Getter method.

5. Write a method GenerateRandomNumber that generates a random number between 1 and 100 and returns it. HINT: You need to use System.Random class to figure this out.

CHAPTER 6: ARRAYS AND COLLECTIONS

What you will learn in this chapter:

- Introduction to arrays
- Working with arrays
- Introduction to collections (list, dictionary, etc.)

INTRODUCTION TO ARRAYS

An array in C# is a collection of items of the same type stored in contiguous memory locations. Arrays are used to store multiple values in a single variable, rather than declaring separate variables for each value.

To create an array in C#, you use the **new** keyword followed by the type of the array and the size of the array in square brackets. For example:

```
int[] numbers = new int[5];
```

This creates an array of integers with a size of 5. The array is initialized with the default values for the type (0 for integers).

You can also create an array and initialize it with values at the same time using the following syntax:

```
int[] numbers = new int[] { 1, 2, 3, 4, 5 };
```

To access an element of the array, you use the index of the element in square brackets. The index is the position of the element in the array, and **it starts at 0**. For example:

```
int first = numbers[0];
int second = numbers[1];
```

You can also modify the value of an element in the array using the same syntax:

```
numbers[2] = 10;
```

You can also use a loop to iterate through the elements of the array:

```
for (int i = 0; i < numbers.Length; i++)
{
    Console.WriteLine(numbers[i]);
}
```

Here are some examples of arrays for different data types in C#:

Integer array:

```
int[] intArray = { 1, 2, 3, 4, 5 };
```

Float array:

```
float[] floatArray = { 1.1f, 2.2f, 3.3f, 4.4f, 5.5f };
```

String array:

```
string[] stringArray = { "apple", "banana", "cherry", "date" };
```

Boolean array:

```
bool[] boolArray = { true, false, true, true, false };
```

Mixed data type array:

```
object[] mixedArr = {1, 2.2f, "apple", false, new int[] { 1, 2 } };
```

WORKING WITH ARRAYS

Here are some examples that demonstrate how to work with arrays in C#:

Declaring and initializing an array:

```
// Declare an array of integers
int[] intArray;

// Initialize the array with values
intArray = new int[] { 1, 2, 3, 4, 5 };
```

Alternatively, you can declare and initialize the array in a single statement:

```
int[] intArray = { 1, 2, 3, 4, 5 };
```

Accessing array elements:

You can access individual elements of an array using the indexing operator ([]):

```
intArray[0] = 10; // Sets the first element of the array to 10
int x = intArray[1]; // x will be equal to 2
```

Iterating through an array:

You can use a **foreach** loop to iterate through the elements of an array:

```
foreach (int element in intArray)
{
    Console.WriteLine(element);
}
```

This will print the elements of the **intArray** to the console, one per line.

Modifying array size:

You can use the **Array.Resize** method to change the size of an array:

```
// Increase the size of the array by 2
Array.Resize(ref intArray, intArray.Length + 2);
```

Note that this will not preserve the values of the original array - any new elements added to the array will be initialized to their default values. We covered default values in an earlier chapter.

EXERCISE SET 1 (ARRAYS)

Here are a few exercises you can try to practice working with arrays in C#:

1. Create an array of integers and print out the sum of all the elements in the array.

2. Given an array of strings, sort the array in alphabetical order.

3. Write a program that finds the second highest number in an array of integers.

4. Write a program that checks if a given string is a palindrome (a word that is spelled the same forwards and backwards).

5. Given an array of integers, create a new array that contains the elements in the original array, but in reverse order.

COLLECTIONS (LIST, DICTIONARY, ETC.)

In C#, a collection is a class that provides a way to store a group of related objects. There are several different types of collections available in the .NET Framework, each with its own specific characteristics and behavior. Some common types of collections in C# include:

- Array: A fixed-size collection of items of the same type.
- List: A dynamic collection of items that can be accessed by index.
- Queue: A first-in, first-out collection of items.
- Stack: A last-in, first-out collection of items.
- Dictionary: A collection of key-value pairs, where each key is unique.

Collections can be useful when you need to store and manipulate a group of related objects, because they provide a number of built-in methods and properties that make it easy to add, remove, and access the items in the collection. They also offer a number of options for customizing their behavior, such as specifying the type of objects that can be added to the collection, or setting the maximum size of the collection.

We have already studied arrays, so let's move on to the rest of the collections.

LIST

A List in C# is a generic collection that provides a resizable array for storing a group of items. Lists are a useful alternative to arrays when you need to add, remove, or access items from a collection, because they offer a number of built-in methods and properties that make it easy to manipulate the items in the list.

Here is an example of how you can use a List in C#:

```csharp
using System.Collections.Generic;

// Create a new List of strings
List<string> names = new List<string>();

// Add some items to the list
names.Add("Alice");
names.Add("Bob");
names.Add("Charlie");

// Access an item in the list by index
string firstName = names[0]; // "Alice"

// Remove an item from the list
names.Remove("Bob");

// Insert an item at a specific index
names.Insert(1, "Bob");

// Find the index of an item in the list
int index = names.IndexOf("Charlie"); // 2

// Check if the list contains a specific item
bool containsCharlie = names.Contains("Charlie"); // true

// Iterate over the items in the list
foreach (string name in names)
{
    Console.WriteLine(name);
}
```

Here are a few practical ways you might use Lists in C#:

1. Storing a list of items that need to be displayed in a user interface, such as a list of products or a list of tasks.
2. Keeping track of a list of objects that need to be updated or processed, such as a list of users or a list of transactions.
3. Storing a list of data that needs to be accessed by index, such as a list of messages or a list of records.
4. Implementing a simple undo/redo system by storing the state of an application in a list.
5. Storing a list of objects that need to be serialized or deserialized, such as a list of settings or a list of objects in a game.

QUEUE

A Queue is a collection in C# that works on the principle of first-in, first-out (FIFO). This means that the first element added to the queue will be the first one to be removed. Queues are often used to store data that needs to be processed in a specific order, or to store tasks that need to be completed in the order they were received.

Here is an example of how you can use a Queue in C#:

```
using System.Collections;

// Create a new Queue
Queue queue = new Queue();
```

```csharp
// Enqueue some items onto the queue
queue.Enqueue("item1");
queue.Enqueue("item2");
queue.Enqueue("item3");

// Check the item at the front of the queue (without dequeuing it)
string front = (string)queue.Peek(); // "item1"

// Dequeue an item from the front of the queue
string item = (string)queue.Dequeue(); // "item1"

// Check the number of items in the queue
int count = queue.Count; // 2

// Iterate over the items in the queue
foreach (string item in queue)
{
    Console.WriteLine(item);
}
```

Here are a few practical ways you might use a Queue in C#:

1. Storing a list of tasks that need to be completed in the order they were received, such as a list of jobs in a print queue or a list of requests in a web server.

2. Keeping track of a list of objects that need to be updated or processed, such as a list of users or a list of transactions.

3. Storing a list of data that needs to be accessed in a first-in, first-out order, such as a list of messages or a list of records.

4. Implementing a simple cache by storing a limited number of items in a queue and removing the oldest items as needed.

5. Storing a list of items that need to be displayed in a user interface, such as a list of notifications or a list of alerts.

STACK

A Stack is a collection in C# that works on the principle of last-in, first-out (LIFO). This means that the last element added to the stack will be the first one to be removed. Stacks are often used to store data in a temporary, undoable buffer, such as the history of visited web pages in a web browser. Imagine that you have a stack of suitcases in the trunk of your car. When you take them out, the suitcase that you put in last will be the first one that you take out. This is exactly how a stack works in C#.

Here is an example of how you can use a Stack in C#:

```
using System.Collections;

// Create a new Stack
Stack stack = new Stack();

// Push some items onto the stack
stack.Push("item1");
stack.Push("item2");
stack.Push("item3");

// Check the top item on the stack (without removing it)
string top = (string)stack.Peek(); // "item3"

// Pop an item off the top of the stack
string item = (string)stack.Pop(); // "item3"

// Check the number of items in the stack
int count = stack.Count; // 2

// Iterate over the items in the stack
foreach (string item in stack)
{
    Console.WriteLine(item);
}
```

Here are a few practical ways you might use a Stack in C#:

1. Implementing an undo/redo system by storing the state of an application in a stack.

2. Storing a list of items that need to be processed in a specific order, such as a list of tasks or a list of events.

3. Keeping track of a list of objects that need to be updated or processed, such as a list of users or a list of transactions.

4. Storing a list of data that needs to be accessed in a last-in, first-out order, such as a list of messages or a list of records.

5. Implementing a simple cache by storing a limited number of items in a stack and removing the oldest items as needed.

DICTIONARY

A Dictionary is a collection in C# that stores a group of key-value pairs, where each key is unique. Dictionaries are useful when you need to store and retrieve data based on a unique identifier, such as a product code or employee ID.

Here is an example of how you can use a Dictionary in C#:

```
using System.Collections.Generic;

// Create a new Dictionary
Dictionary<string, int> dictionary = new Dictionary<string, int>();

// Add some key-value pairs to the dictionary
dictionary.Add("apple", 1);
dictionary.Add("banana", 2);
dictionary.Add("cherry", 3);

// Check if the dictionary contains a specific key
bool containsApple = dictionary.ContainsKey("apple"); // true

// Access the value for a specific key
int appleValue = dictionary["apple"]; // 1

// Change the value for a specific key
dictionary["apple"] = 4;
```

```
// Remove a key-value pair from the dictionary
dictionary.Remove("cherry");

// Iterate over the key-value pairs in the dictionary
foreach (KeyValuePair<string, int> pair in dictionary)
{
    Console.WriteLine($"{pair.Key}: {pair.Value}");
}
```

Here are a few practical ways you might use dictionaries in C#:

1. Storing user profiles or other records that need to be accessed by a unique identifier, such as a username or ID number.
2. Mapping product codes to product names or descriptions in an e-commerce application.
3. Storing translations of words or phrases in multiple languages.
4. Caching frequently used data to improve the performance of an application.
5. Storing configurations or settings for an application in a key-value format.

EXERCISE SET 2 (COLLECTIONS)

Here are a few exercises you can try to practice working with various types of collections in C#:

1. Create a program that stores a list of names in an array, and then allows the user to add and remove names from the list.

2. Write a program that stores a history of visited web pages in a stack, and allows the user to navigate back and forth through the history.

3. Create a program that stores a list of tasks in a queue, and allows the user to add and remove tasks from the list.

4. Write a program that stores a dictionary of student grades, where the keys are the student names and the values are their grades. Allow the user to add, update, and remove students from the dictionary.

5. Create a program that stores a list of contacts in a list, and allows the user to search for a contact by name or phone number.

CHAPTER 7: EXCEPTION HANDLING

What you will learn in this chapter:
- What are exceptions?
- Try-catch-finally blocks
- Throwing exceptions

WHAT ARE EXCEPTIONS?

There once was a brilliant programmer named Jane who created a top-of-the-line scientific calculator. It could perform all sorts of calculations with ease and accuracy, and Jane was proud of her creation. She made it available as a web application and it quickly gained a large user base of students from all around the world.

One day, a student named John tried to use the calculator to solve a particularly tricky equation. He typed in the numbers and symbols, hit the "enter" button, and waited for the result. But instead of the expected answer, an error message popped up on his screen. The program had crashed!

John was frustrated and confused. He had no idea what had gone wrong or how to fix it. Luckily, Jane had anticipated this possibility and had implemented something called "exception handling" in her program.

When an error occurred, the calculator would catch it, display a helpful message to John, and allow him to try again with the correct input. This way, the program could continue running smoothly and not cause any more frustration for its users.

Thanks to exception handling, John was able to quickly correct his mistake and get the correct result from the calculator. He was grateful to Jane for her foresight and careful programming, and the scientific calculator remained a beloved and useful tool for students everywhere.

Exception handling is a mechanism in C# that allows you to handle runtime errors or unexpected conditions in your code. When an exception is thrown, it disrupts the normal flow of execution and can cause your program to crash. Exception handling allows you to catch and handle these exceptions in a controlled manner, so that you can either fix the problem or gracefully terminate the program.

At a high level, exception handling in C# consists of two main parts: throwing an exception and catching an exception.

Throwing an exception involves using the **throw** keyword to create and throw an exception object when an error or unexpected condition occurs. The exception object contains information about the error, such as the type of error and a description of the problem.

Catching an exception involves using a **try** block to enclose the code that might throw an exception, and a **catch** block to handle the exception if it is thrown. The **catch** block contains the code that will be executed when an exception is thrown, and can optionally include a variable to hold the exception object.

In C#, there are several types of exceptions that you can throw and catch, including system-defined exceptions and custom exceptions that you define yourself. You can also use the **finally** block to specify code that should always be executed, whether an exception is thrown or not.

I hope this high-level overview of exception handling in C# is helpful! Let me know if you have any questions or if you'd like more information.

TRY-CATCH-FINALLY BLOCKS

In C#, a **try-catch** block is a way to handle exceptions that might be thrown during the execution of your code. The **try** block encloses the code that might throw an exception, and the **catch** block contains the code that will be executed if an exception is thrown.

Here is an example of a **try-catch** block in C#:

```
try
{
    // Code that might throw an exception goes here
}
catch (Exception ex)
{
    // Code to handle the exception goes here
}
```

You can use multiple **catch** blocks to handle different types of exceptions, or you can use a **catch** block with a specific exception type to handle that type of exception. For example:

```
try
{
    // Code that might throw an exception goes here
}
catch (ArgumentException ex)
{
    // Code to handle ArgumentException goes here
}
catch (Exception ex)
{
    // Code to handle other types of exceptions goes here
}
```

You can also use the **finally** block to specify code that should always be executed, whether an exception is thrown or not. For example:

```
try
{
    // Code that might throw an exception goes here
}
catch (Exception ex)
{
    // Code to handle the exception goes here
}
finally
{
    // Code to be executed regardless of whether an exception was thrown goes here
}
```

Here are a few concrete examples of **try-catch** blocks in C#:

1. Handling a divide-by-zero error:

```
try
{
    int x = 5;
    int y = 0;
    int result = x / y;
}
catch (DivideByZeroException ex)
{
    Console.WriteLine("Error: Cannot divide by zero.");
}
```

2. Reading a file and handling a file not found error:

```
try
{
    string fileContents = File.ReadAllText("file.txt");
    Console.WriteLine(fileContents);
}
catch (FileNotFoundException ex)
{
    Console.WriteLine("Error: File not found.");
}
```

3. Parsing a string to an integer and handling a format exception:

```
try
{
    string input = "abc";
    int number = int.Parse(input);
    Console.WriteLine(number);
}
catch (FormatException ex)
{
    Console.WriteLine("Error: Invalid format.");
}
```

THROWING EXCEPTIONS

In C#, you can throw an exception using the **throw** keyword to indicate that an error or unexpected condition has occurred. You can throw a system-defined exception or create a custom exception by instantiating an exception object and providing a message to describe the error.

Here are a few practical examples of throwing exceptions in C#:

1. Throwing a system-defined exception when an invalid argument is passed to a method:

```csharp
public void SetValue(int x)
{
    if (x < 0)
    {
        throw new ArgumentException("x must be greater than or equal to zero.");
    }
    this.value = x;
}
```

2. Throwing a custom exception when a file is not found:

```csharp
public string ReadFile(string fileName)
{
    if (!File.Exists(fileName))
    {
        throw new FileNotFoundException("File not found.", fileName);
    }
    return File.ReadAllText(fileName);
}
```

3. Throwing an exception when an object is in an invalid state:

```csharp
public void ProcessData()
{
    if (data == null)
    {
        throw new InvalidOperationException("data is null.");
    }
    // Process the data
}
```

Exception handling is a way to handle runtime errors and unexpected situations in C# programming. Understanding the basics of exception handling is important, but there is more to learn. To get a deeper understanding, I recommend looking at various online resources, such as tutorials and documentation. Some good places to start include:

- The official C# documentation on exception handling: https://docs.microsoft.com/en-us/dotnet/csharp/programming-guide/exceptions/

- A tutorial on exception handling in C# from Microsoft: https://docs.microsoft.com/en-us/dotnet/csharp/tutorials/exception-handling

- A tutorial on exception handling in C# from the C# Programming Yellow Book: https://www.csharpstar.com/csharp-exception-handling/

These resources will provide you with a solid foundation in exception handling in C#, including how to catch and handle exceptions, how to throw custom exceptions, and how to use the **try**, **catch**, and **finally** blocks to structure your exception handling code.

EXERCISES

Here are a few exercises you can try to practice exception handling in C#:

1. Write a program that reads a list of integers from a file and adds them together. Handle any exceptions that might be thrown when trying to read the file or parse the integers.

2. Create a program that prompts the user for a file name and reads the contents of the file. If the file is not found, prompt the user to enter a new file name.

3. Write a program that divides two numbers entered by the user. If the user tries to divide by zero, display an error message.

4. Create a program that reads a list of names from a file and stores them in a list. If the file is not found, create a new file and write the names to the file.

5. Write a program that prompts the user for a number and displays the corresponding day of the week (e.g. 1 for Monday, 2 for Tuesday, etc.). If the user enters an invalid number, display an error message.

CHAPTER 8: FINAL PROJECT (SIMPLE CONSOLE GAME)

What you will learn in this chapter:
- Planning and designing your game
- Implementing your game in C#
- Adding polish and finishing touches

PLANNING AND DESIGNING YOUR GAME

Here is a simple console game that you could use to practice your C# skills: Rock-paper-scissors. This classic game involves two players choosing either rock, paper, or scissors. The winner is determined by the rules: rock beats scissors, scissors beats paper, and paper beats rock. You can create a program that allows the user to play against the computer, or against another player. To start, you can create a program that allows the user to enter their choice (rock, paper, or scissors) and displays the result of the game. You can then expand the program by adding a loop to allow the user to play multiple rounds, and by keeping track of the score.

Here is some sample code to get you started:

```
while (true)
{
    Console.WriteLine("Enter your choice
                      (rock, paper, or scissors):");
    string userChoice = Console.ReadLine();

    // Generate a random choice for the computer
    Random random = new Random();
    int computerChoice = random.Next(3);
```

```csharp
        string[] choices = { "rock", "paper", "scissors" };
        string computerChoiceString = choices[computerChoice];

        // Determine the winner
        if (userChoice == computerChoiceString)
        {
            Console.WriteLine("Tie!");
        }
        else if ((userChoice == "rock"
                    && computerChoiceString == "scissors") ||
                (userChoice == "scissors"
                    && computerChoiceString == "paper") ||
                (userChoice == "paper"
                    && computerChoiceString == "rock"))
        {
            Console.WriteLine("You win!");
        }
        else
        {
            Console.WriteLine("You lose!");
        }
    }
}
```

IMPLEMENTING YOUR GAME IN C#

1. Try implementing the code for the entire game on your own.

2. Get the basic functionality working with each run of the program implementing one game.

3. Extend the program to play multiple times and keep a score board. Use an indefinite while loop and a switch statement to evaluate choices.

ADDING POLISH AND FINISHING TOUCHES

1. Implement exception handling for user input

2. Store the results in a new file when exiting the program

3. Use collections to keep track of the score board

YOUR TICKET TO A BRIGHT FUTURE

NOTE: Please try to implement the solution on your own before looking at the solution below

Here is the complete game code for a rock-paper-scissors game in C#:

```csharp
using System;
using System.Collections.Generic;
using System.Linq;
using System.Text;
using System.Threading.Tasks;

namespace RockPaperScissors
{
    class Program
    {
        static void Main(string[] args)
        {
            int userWins = 0;
            int computerWins = 0;
            int ties = 0;

            while (true)
            {
                Console.WriteLine("Enter your choice (rock, paper, or scissors):");
                string userChoice = Console.ReadLine();

                // Generate a random choice for the computer
                Random random = new Random();
                int computerChoice = random.Next(3);
                string[] choices = { "rock", "paper", "scissors" };
                string computerChoiceString = choices[computerChoice];

                // Determine the winner
                if (userChoice == computerChoiceString)
                {
                    Console.WriteLine("Tie!");
                    ties++;
                }
                else if ((userChoice == "rock" && computerChoiceString == "scissors") ||
                         (userChoice == "scissors" && computerChoiceString == "paper") ||
                         (userChoice == "paper" && computerChoiceString == "rock"))
                {
                    Console.WriteLine("You win!");
                    userWins++;
                }
                else
                {
```

```csharp
                Console.WriteLine("You lose!");
                computerWins++;
            }

            Console.WriteLine("Score: You {0} - {1} Computer",
userWins, computerWins);
        }
      }
    }
}
```

Here's the program with all the bell and whistles:

```csharp
using System;
using System.Collections.Generic;
using System.Linq;
using System.Text;
using System.Threading.Tasks;

namespace RockPaperScissors
{
  class Program
  {
    static void Main(string[] args)
    {
      Dictionary<string, int> scoreBoard = new Dictionary<string, int>();
      scoreBoard["user"] = 0;
      scoreBoard["computer"] = 0;
      scoreBoard["tie"] = 0;

      while (true)
      {
        Console.WriteLine("Menu:");
        Console.WriteLine("1. Play game");
        Console.WriteLine("2. Display score");
        Console.WriteLine("3. Exit");
        Console.WriteLine("Enter your choice:");
        string menuChoice = Console.ReadLine();

        try
        {
          switch (int.Parse(menuChoice))
          {
            case 1:
              // Play the game
              Console.WriteLine("Enter your choice (rock, paper, or scissors):");
              string userChoice = Console.ReadLine();

              // Generate a random choice for the computer
              Random random = new Random();
              int computerChoice = random.Next(3);
              string[] choices = { "rock", "paper", "scissors" };
```

```csharp
            string computerChoiceString = choices[computerChoice];

            // Determine the winner
            if (userChoice == computerChoiceString)
            {
              Console.WriteLine("Tie!");
              scoreBoard["tie"]++;
            }
            else if ((userChoice == "rock" && computerChoiceString == "scissors") ||
                     (userChoice == "scissors" && computerChoiceString == "paper") ||
                     (userChoice == "paper" && computerChoiceString == "rock"))
            {
              Console.WriteLine("You win!");
              scoreBoard["user"]++;
            }
            else
            {
              Console.WriteLine("You lose!");
              scoreBoard["computer"]++;
            }
            break;

          case 2:
            // Display the score
            Console.WriteLine("Score: You {0} - {1} Computer", scoreBoard["user"], scoreBoard["computer"]);
            Console.WriteLine("Ties: {0}", scoreBoard["tie"]);
            break;

          case 3:
            // Exit the program
            // TODO: Save the score board to a new file (named score_<timestamp>.txt)
            return;

          default:
            Console.WriteLine("Invalid choice. Please try again.");
            break;
        }
      }
      catch (FormatException ex)
      {
        Console.WriteLine("Error parsing user input!");
        Console.WriteLine(ex.Message);
      }
    }
  }
}
```

ANDY V

CHAPTER 9: MORE PROJECTS

One of the most effective ways to learn to program is by actively practicing and applying the concepts you have learned. This is similar to going to the gym and lifting weights to build muscle strength. Repeatedly applying the language constructs through coding exercises helps to reinforce your understanding and improve your ability to translate logical thinking into code.

This is a list of projects you can use to practice and reinforce the concepts and skills you have learned in your course. By working on these projects and implementing solutions in code, you will have the opportunity to further understand and solidify your understanding of the material.

Some of them are repeats but get through them in sequential order.

PRACTICE PROJECTS – SET 1 (EASY)

4. Hello World: Create a simple program that displays "Hello, World!" on the screen. This is a classic first program that helps beginners understand the basic structure of a C# program.

5. Calculator: Create a simple calculator that can perform basic arithmetic operations (addition, subtraction, multiplication, and division).

6. Tic-Tac-Toe: Create a simple Tic-Tac-Toe game that can be played between two players.

7. Hangman: Create a simple hangman game where the user has to guess a word within a certain number of tries.

8. Rock, Paper, Scissors: Create a simple Rock, Paper, Scissors game that can be played against the computer.

9. Blackjack: Create a simple Blackjack game where the player competes against the computer.

10. To-Do List: Create a simple to-do list program where the user can add and remove items from a list.

11. BMI Calculator: Create a program that calculates the body mass index (BMI) of a person based on their height and weight.

12. Temperature Converter: Create a program that converts temperatures between Celsius and Fahrenheit.

13. Employee Management System: Create a program that allows a user to manage a list of employees, including adding new employees, editing existing employees, and deleting employees.

PRACTICE PROJECTS – SET 2 (MEDIUM TO HARD)

1. **Student Grades:** Create a program that allows a teacher to enter student grades for a course and calculates the average, minimum, and maximum grade.

2. **Inventory Manager:** Create a program that allows a user to manage an inventory of products, including adding new products, updating existing products, and deleting products.

3. **Banking System:** Create a program that simulates a simple banking system, allowing users to open new accounts, make deposits and withdrawals, and check their balance.

4. **Media Library:** Create a program that allows a user to manage a library of media, including books, movies, and music. The program should allow the user to add new items, check out and return items, and see a list of items currently checked out.

5. **Recipe Database:** Create a program that allows a user to store and manage a collection of recipes. The program should allow the user to add new recipes, view existing recipes, and delete recipes.

6. **Quiz Game:** Create a program that generates a quiz for the user and allows them to answer multiple-choice questions. The program should keep track of the user's score and provide feedback after each question.

7. Sudoku: Create a program that generates and solves Sudoku puzzles.

8. File Encryption/Decryption: Create a program that allows a user to encrypt and decrypt files using a password.

9. Text Adventure: Create a simple text-based adventure game where the user can make choices and explore a virtual world.

10. Image Viewer: Create a program that allows a user to view and manage a collection of images. The program should allow the user to view images, rotate them, and delete them.